RAIN CYCLE

Robin Lodewick, Age 9

RAIN CYCLE

Robin Brant Lodwick

lone goose press
eugene, oregon

Linocut on facing page by Robin Lodewick.

Drawings of penstemons on pages 2, 27, and 59 by Robin Brant Lodewick. They are from *A Descriptive Key to Oregon Penstemons* by Robin Lodewick, Native Plant Society of Oregon Publication, 1994.

LCCN: 2015954816

ISBN: 978-0-9905950-2-1

First Edition

Designed by Sandy Tilcock

Contents

I am What That Horizon Says to Me

Robin Brant Lodewick, 1923-2014

Artist, self-educated naturalist, bibliophile, keen observer of both human interactions and the realm of insects, wildflowers, rocks and raptors, Robin Lodewick pursued the craft of poetry with fierce dedication. Though her work was largely unpublished in her lifetime, she specified in her will that a collection of her poems be made available to the public through libraries across the country. She perceived these writings to be part of her legacy and wished to share them with whoever cared to enter into the complex, quirky world of her expression.

Born in 1923, Robin Brant was home-schooled by her mother Hazeldean Brant, an editor of children's books. Her father, Irving Brant, was a journalist, editor and author. Among other works, he published a major multiple-volume biography of James Madison over several decades, starting in 1941. Robin's family placed a high value on the arts, intellectual curiosity, environmental concerns and humanitarian issues. Her father's career took the family on many travels. In addition to providing academic grounding, her home-based education embraced camping and hiking as the family explored mountains, deserts, prairies and canyons across the continent.

Robin obtained a high school diploma at age 16 by "testing out". She attended the Corcoran Gallery School of Art in Washington, DC, and later, Pratt Institute of Art in Brooklyn, NY.

Robin wrote and illustrated two unpublished books: *Chum*, a children's book, and *Hawk Mountain*, an educational essay honoring a sanctuary for birds of prey in Pennsylvania. She also illustrated two books her father published for young people. Robin read widely, with insatiable curiosity. Her passion for books led her to library work, and in 1960 she took a position at the University of Oregon Library in Eugene, which she held until her retirement in 1981.

In Eugene, Robin became involved in outdoor and environmental organizations. It was through one of these groups that she met Ken Lodewick, a highway engineer, builder and amateur botanist who shared her passion for wild-flowers and close observation of the dynamics of the natural world. They married in 1963 and remained together until Ken's death in 2012. They were active in a number of organizations including The Obsidians, The Rock Garden Society, The Penstemon Society and Mt. Pisgah Arboretum. Robin and Ken became known as experts on the penstemons and referred to themselves as "penstemaniacs". The co-authored several scholarly articles on the genus, and on the history of botanical discovery and classification in the Northwest. Those who knew the Lodewicks came to respect them for their generosity, their integrity and the pure devotion they brought to both their scientific and creative pursuits.

While Robin had written poetry earlier in her life, it was in Eugene in the early 1960's that she began to pursue this form of expression with particular passion and determination. In plain, blunt language and with a restless imagination, she sought to probe the deepest questions of human identity and experience, nature, history and evolution, Some of her poems are very personal. Many stem from being present in natural landscapes, or respond to a scientific study.

The editor has selected and arranged Robin's poems in three groups, somewhat arbitrarily. The first group, primarily of a personal nature, includes serious and not-so-serious works, love poems, a meditation on the death of a child, and reflections on aging. Here you will find a poem Robin had written at age 5 and took pains to preserve among her writings. It also includes a prose poem based on the historical figure Thomas Cranmer and a valiant, though perhaps unsuccessful, attempt to disprove the assertion that English has no rhyme for the word "orange". The second set includes poems rooted in nature, and the third embraces those that engage a philosophical or metaphysical perspective.

Robin Lodewick made extensive use of a compound form that, if she did not invent, she certainly molded into her own mode of expression. She refers to poems in this form as "glozed poems". A poetic narration on the left side of the page is accompanied by a spare, aphoristic poem on the right side, its lines connecting with selected lines of the original poem. In a note accompanying one of these poems, she states that the two poems are to be read separately, then together. It is not entirely clear how the "together" version is to be understood. In some cases, incorporating the words of the right-side poem into the lines of the left poem to which they correspond results in a changed or amplified sense. In other cases this does not seem to apply. The editor believes that one way in which these poems would "work" is to have two readers perform the left and right poems simultaneously, preserving the continuity of each part. Interpenetration appears to be a signal feature of these poems: interpenetration of natural events, lives, ideas, perceptions. "Rain Cycle", whose title was borrowed to name this collection, is among the wildest and most puzzling of Robin's poems. The bewildering constructions with multiple parenthetical insertions, linking galaxies, birds, oceans and the reader, suggest that she is striving to capture in language the complex intertwinings she glimpsed in nature.

In her poetry, Robin sought to challenge both herself and the reader. Alongside her earthy realism and the often complex churn of ideas she invokes, there is reverence and affection for the natural world, and an appreciation for the mysteries of being human.

Patrick Tilcock, Editor
Eugene, Oregon, 2015

A Sort of Music

Penstemon Deustus

Silence

Weighted by death
I can raise
joy;
surrounded
by a fringe
of trouble,
glow green
with grass
and not be
jealous
or mold.
Since the business
of poetry is to combine
incompatibles
it comes best
to one who is sick,
getting up;
or healthy, and falling.
Real endings
like long happiness
do no suit.
Therefore, mixing
bad with good
I hedge
all my weddings
make a
sort of music

and cling on.
Complete giving
away of self
would mean such deep
silence
after the pain
had gone over,
and the abyss
of moonlight
opened
upon
our peace.

Apology

The photographer, loading red peppers
into a grocery sack, said Hello
to his mother's friend. The old woman,
waiting for her clerk, shook hands
then asked, Do you
work here now? While thinking, does
this boy look like his father (or could it
be another brother?) He
went off, confused; she stayed, still
mixed-up. It would have
made more sense to say, How's
Outer Mongolia doing? No, actually . . .
but that might have boggled every
body else in store. (Did the Gobi
dessicate skin of its mummy
so fast between click/snap
as to leave no greeny film
tombed in its stone, or now to be
drunk into bone?) Thirty years
from now you'll understand, young man
(who's 40ish? 50ish?) what I've
just learned. Keep one thing
in mind, don't conflate a second
or a third (that way,
poetry lies). My best friend says
No one knows how to answer
the weird things you come up with,

then will not talk to me
for a month, until I
(she) go, I miss you, and she
(I) I too. That's plain. But this
curse of double vision between
brain cell and sight … no wonder it's
so seldom that our facts and the blue
sky (drizzle?) of stopped motion, blurred
friendship or word-making meet. On
crowded slopes, where carfuls of
flowers head off for wedding-funerals
or for the poppy-factory, only blind
worm, cave fishes can avoid
enigma: to be Oneself, and not be
Other.

For Matthew at 8 Months

Nothing's wrong   with the earth   Single
death won't cure;   over stone and
green, rain   (under fur's   life's
skin, pain).   No future comes   out of
for those alive,   but that was so
eons ago.   Why should knowing   whole;
sight still can be,   help me? Yet
friend's child   who may have then   never
have felt unknown wind,   black sun, let's
remember now.   At each ending   same
red twig, crow caw,   moving trees'
tops make spring.   Even when   wavering
old buries young,   rust's left
licheny vent.   Pink of
some cell, opening,   splits; another   doubled
cycle out from ocean,   drums   within
on ground.   Stoned bone, lighted
atoms across void   create   Flame.
Bang,   again.

God Head

I'm trying to say that you're
in me love, you're in me very
deep. In don't mean sex or flesh
or food, or any child. But you
are what I grow my ways around,
in, underneath. Beyond,
the lights on surface area the mind's fears'
flux. They don't apply.
You may be good or bad, and I
adult or sullen, pecking at
your wish. What counts
in what one writes stems from
a country that is equally unknown.
Full comfort there, the bulk
that may be fallen back on if
one does not look, the solid
not-me of the core.
It need not be a joy; it's felt
by default, not by hurt. Here
faith is out of place, and other frets
are not involved. I've no
thing there that is myself
to fear. Nor are you with me
there. The one we speak of even
can no more exist
where persons fail.
Safe, fool, at last

where God is
nothing, but he
Is.

Menopause

It is a coffin not a womb I bear,
with no expansion. Yet my dear
this must be held to, that the grey
rain-drive August end which sees
old year come on to us again
is what is given. In your hands
even what you deny hangs fruitful
and the skill, the husbanding I feel
now side by side, makes gravel rise
cracking sterility. That grave's
rose decking is ersatz, wet card;
its bells, its wedding bands and rings
fall all to heap. But wrong
choice is not made, we live absurd
or sordid; our disease manhood, our
curing in the ground, or we
march on. No spring remains, no surer
summer for a childhood to revive, high
tasseled, awkward in the joint and fair
for harvest. In the empty house
I hear your feet, your voice out of the walls
that are blank now. Oh love, be all
that I may carry, be my son, not spouse.

Molly and the Garbage Can
(written in 1928 at age 5)

Molly wanted to eat the garbage can.
The garbage can wanted to eat Molly.
She went over and ate it;
She ate the face, she ate the lid, she ate
The body.
Then her mother took her around and
Showed people, and they threw things in.
When she was full she stood on her head
And it all fell out.
Not the can though. It was stuck too tight.

Critical Words
(which any critic is entitled to take personally)

Don't do it to me, you   Long after,
(future) fooling even now
with meanings I can't find,
put in by being forced to. Here's   later,
someone seeing through another's
set of eyelids, using "me, a
friend" for hidey-
hole, in, under, out of   Words
limestone layers or
brain's skull, until
we each find other's roots
at the cave's end. Which   (stalactites'
(ahead, descending) point us   pillars, cracked
back up toward sky, connecting
tongue, womb, and cells   at gravity's top
with what comes out of   summit)
them, beyond day's
peak or century's
banging. Past   (winged
all-fall-off of water-
flow, sand's circular   fingerings,
blowings at tipped edge have   fluttering)
got to bridge us forward so
(what eye? what I?) may yet
get to meanings (more,   plummet
as always, the more ears
we hear by) through these

heaped up, have-to-publish
sounds (forever spouted, spilled)   down onto ground:
by profs, men-husbands,
lover-boys—those very souls   the atoms we're
(oh, babies) I'm
responsible for.   to reassemble.

Toward '04

All is healed, all is whole, all's
well; over there, through the trees, water
falls, from, into wells. Fiery red-
orange spills, out of summer's burning
to be lightnesses of white. Past years that
hover (over chaos? over child? whether
still undying or not yet alive) what's
come shall go, through doors no power
closes and no hand undoes. Shone onto
in mind's wind, wind's mind, we'll
search old earth's cover for its
petaled seed, bone-needled and odd-
egged, so quickening toward east
sun's rise (blackened at back). Oh,
good morrow, sister, and
be kind, my mother, don't delay
to cry at borning, call out joy, succor
future. Let me save, in you, my selves,
in me, all our returnings, prove
by next creation's green, world's Word's
beyond now whirled.

Cranmer

Carried slightly on the forward edge of what to me is time,
to others simply motion toward, never back and down;
with Goethe crying in his great dead cavern of a brain, more light
(that did not come by any sun we've seen, behind his lids
to show thin figures), with him and other I intend to stay
my classic aging, as two thousand centuries end.
Rouse, Pythagoras, you shall see unmoving beauty bare
her unity, of one or zero; Bodhisattvas, die in a like
centered naught. Under the stars that may remain when eyer
has shut shop and wandered home, under the love that can
not be assumed, sit down to journey. Unembalmed
and not in charity banked-on, to be the muscle in another's
later self, not furnishing historians' future or their dim
trust in past, unpeaceful, under power we throw
up our dead. Sprawled, making the sunsets red
to color-blinded charred earth film, the soil's gone back
for a fresh start in unammoniac seas. Why, dear,
fair and foolish man, must you go down to grave with all
your wives and cows and such a banging, are the drums
of daybreak and nightfall not enough? What lack
set lightly on the upcurved and downrushing wall
(which precedes Sol, which ends man's time, and men's)
what pride has brought us to millennium?
Waste guilt; we attempted not to yield, to win
for further suns, undying willed-to-generations eyes, souls
that could climb skies. Ah love, what loss.
The exhausted ship sets down, into its own tail fire.

The Übermensch sighs, dies. Our potter's field gets tears,
or comets, onto it, and then the fallacy of pathos goes out too.
One person only, a Quixote, has signed himself with laughter
to the still blank blinking site, this corner of the heavens
that is hot, bright; dark and dwarfish; having
a signal yet to do, a wave, or mental particle directed out.
Now folly of creation, since we've made us or we were made fit
to joke at fizzle, know: You cannot derogate or make recant,
more that might of Christendom could Joan, what, wrecked,
is not I, and, unburned, goes running to the stake.

Editor's note: English cleric Thomas Cranmer (1489-1556) was Archbishop
of Canterbury during the reigns of Henry VIII. Edward VI and Mary I. He
was a central figure in the complex, often bloody doctrinal and political struggles
that established the Church of England. He often took a progressive and conciliatory
role. With the accession of the Roman Catholic Mary I, he was among those
condemned to death for heresy. Although he recanted his reformist views, he
withdrew his recantation on the day of his execution.

Orangeless
**There is no rhyme in English
for the word "orange".**

Orangeless
in Los Angeles
our whore, Angie,
flew off to the
(possibly) orangier
(though mangier)
Ganges, there found
a vendor of stranger
fruit for her porringer
than apple or orange or
plum. "Bum" lunged her
tongue at him, "I'll
arrange yer
sporangia
for ya." Down-cringing
the frangi-
ble guru cried "Orgy on
otherwhere, Madam,
oh, range
farther"; angelic, a
messenger (harbinger
of calm) then descended,
or our Angelica
would have gone for her
derringer.
Wiser (but
grungier)

Annie's returning
home to Tangiers
(Utah) where engin-
eers shout,
urging her
on (her own G-
string, in future,
to be
Red).

Oregon Geology: an Ode

Syndepositional chronostratigraphy shows an
aseismic subsidence during paleoliquifaction,
while evidence of strong shaking from cobble
plumes, basal shears or lateral spreads indicates
formation of clastic dikes and abundant sills
        (Dikes and sills)
after fluidization, as entrained (disoriented)
sand clads invade the hosting duodeposits.

On the other hand, erosionally truncated
convolute beds prove multiple liquefaction
events occurred, within the period of marine
highstand, as do the accreting wedges in fold
and thrust belts, associated with fluidized dune
        (Fold and thrust)
crossbedding of bench laminations that surround
sand blows or boils, and the fissures above dike,
sill, and flume.
        (Seismic blows, boils and flumes)

Quotations from "The Ore-Bin," the former newsletter
of the State Department of Geology, with the addition of
twenty short words including "On the other hand."

Bog

On the edge of death of walking
things and buds, that bundle
out of bark (afterward the wings
will be left ooze) we huddle
watching birds. At eighty-nine,
if my mind knows anything , it treadles
on a disintegrating log, not down
stream into roar, but sog. Contraction
can't begin to pay youth's earth
the upsrung joy we've taken
and drunk grave for, rather
junkpiling cars, wars, stars
than to choose drought, than dearth.
Still, holding in, the trees
and those who've shut their cells
by a brain stroke, skills
likewise hulled, can green, dream
a catastrophe, not to close shop
too soon. Better mad men
blame God's bad mud? For evolution's stop
or solve own evil: boom.
Flying, juncos maintain
something remains, sky mends
after sun ends.

Gold Point

You must resolve in mind to add
these yellows to the blue of God.
He will not do it, who
splits all. If sound delights you
know, no other likes it so. The clanging
of the spheres is not our harmony.
Why, two souls cannot mesh, but
mutually miss. Perhaps a friction that
Proves isolating skin, makes world.
As one, our beams of colors
would become too white, and quite
unable to be loved, by its
self satisfied. So glitter, break
or cry. The gift from each
to his other is our touch, which
cuts, to ache.

New World

You love me; that is all
the world I have
to live in, give
back, or to hold in my mind's
wall. Against the agony
of night-waked town,
the children with their bony
grinning knives, the red light
sound, you bring a green
globe where right
waxes, fruit
is not decayed. Our lean
gummings in this sooty room
of skull, of city
that is burning, home
to no human who is not here
killed, so ended.
Atrocity is what
he who has not
gets, hopeless for his hoped-for lover.
Ah God, if you'd arranged to be
grace-giver, fewer
of your damned, our
poor, would be engaged
increasing the one thing they know,
their hell. A heaven
that's been shown

me once alone
stays, grow, and lies
ahead, last haven.

The Window on the Garden

Jealous gods will take from us
these leaves, this beauty.
Sun can not be always here
to draw its lines, long,
glowing, from within to out
or scatter green along the paths
from womb to wooer.
No more do lilies and the purple phlox
stay with us; sooner
than you will, the tight heads droop
to dung-gathering ground.
In heaps the old-age-freckled, cream
and tinted girls recline,
a bucketful of clipped
hay now. Likewise, I, spreading
my late wishes on this thin
pine-bearing soil, shall see them work
with sureness only in a second
generation seed. Outdoors
there is a coarser air
and rain. You, reaper,
have been common to us
many years; we'll lie
around new roots
more quietly than we rise here
still trembling toward that close.

Weed Into Us Your
Imperfections of the Future

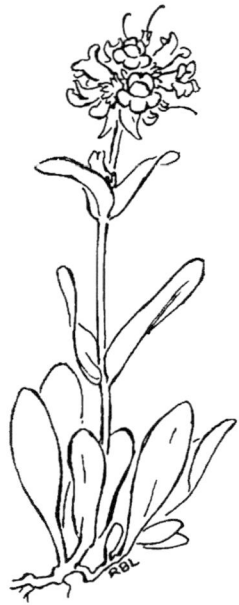

Penstemon Globosus

Ai-ee; O-oo

Light's still between   live red,   Between
dying green,   as plum enters
its March, as fir leaves.   Slim cat   cat, hawk
eternally behind   squirrel, or hawk
photo-op'd above   nest ledge,   above nest,
gets sky-scrapered.   Mankind   man
teeters in own balance,   distressed   (in own
at the leaping germ's   intoxicant
floodings, toward each   sight, fog,   floods, fogs)
vein.   Weed into us your
imperfections of the future,   where   perfecting,
(scarlet, or dried) blood   is to paint   paints
hair, scum,   liming the graced   limed-over
eyes of revelation.   Yet at outer
wall, some   hand's skin touches   wall
to make changeling,   molds form from   (changed from
within. Sloth, tiger,   bug   within,
that buries dung to   its arising, we
all're flesh,   share a beast-morphic   beast-
bottom stratum,   know chemical   layer buried):
that wails, unliking   tooth's truth;   Truths
made by mind,   a speaking (?)   unspoken
floats (bubbles?)   lightly upon inch-deep
cover that's Earth's   sap: the humus   covering
over our eye, ear,   cry.   our Cry.

No Comfort

In heavy circles on broad wings, great hawk   Job's
turns over cemetery hill, (old settlers'
headstones knocked down by new boys
each year, and ivy gone). Our   wives
city has not met such
stiller of what lives below, for long.
above him tilts and spins seagull, a flash,   weep
a scream, in all ways narrower
and whiter, pulled to orbit around
beaked air's core: odd   unchilded
coupling of the unvoiced, loud. To us
jay can say "cat" and run scared, as nestling
tits chase crow; if crows which summer   bodies,
among graveyard firs mob owl, whole
of the town flock comes, caws. But   not
gulls fly high and silver, winters, to the dump,
return at evening in a long V'd line
of sea-sound, carelessly. Does cast-out   word
lost sentry shout her former fears,
or hate, wanting an enemy to answer to—   God
"do not ignore me, for I sin
no more than you"? High preyer,   doesn't speak,
unnoticing, swings on toward river
that flows north. In distance
we see dot, followed by other
dot, hear the faint crying.   whirling.

October Bees

October: bees reveal
that pears are down; the sun
reveals the bees. Sight
of their snowy flight, swooped
across beam shot
through shadow (between
maroon leaves, green) is followed
by zoom down
to darkness under trees'
trunks' drunk fruit-fall.
Here's joy, jobwork, hope
and zing, as living keeps on
with its dying till December cold
has hibernated all our
seeds, buds, bees
for what's as yet unopened:
April—then when whatever souls
are left of us go off
across the reddening roofs
of summer.

Wayside

Bright reflector, green   Gold
beetle, eyes sun from central
fuzz of lily cup. Scabbed   mine's
land put up grey-dawn-pink
scurf out of gravel, to shelter
him; as Earth's plates, fuming   stones
once, now weather cooled, sap
homed. (That buds   (clayed,
could not exist in a young
universe, proves them
to be what's fit, not
it.) Bug,   opening into
camera focused down
at haven, pokes head over
rim, flies off. Day's   wings)
portrait lost, the viewers   shall forever
stand in split between
flip-on of light and its later   end in
darkening, where we've   mankind's
short flutter. Should
blues, leaves continue
rolling under stars, who'd   Bone.
stay to be God,
see?

Companion

What I'd do if I were you
is just what you would do to me,
and if I have a smaller brain
than I had a year ago, how
many others last as well
inside of a cat or a squirrel's skull
instead of this big baboon's?
So sit and look at the sun with me,
bear in your western ridge, and we'll
think with the anthers and petals
of flowers, or the tongueings of second-rate
mates (males, gals). Only the yellowing
lion knows, whose kit is whose (he's
killed all the rest) and our grazers
are led here by cows. So when you go
whack on the back with your
antlers and horns, or roar above
roar in the night, remember
that barely audible softened
purr, lips, claws that retract. Find
fingers' most basic use, of touch;
look, eye to eye, each
into each. Since mind expands
to fill world met, shout
out to companion, whatever's
enough: what's loved
is alive.

April, Opening

Dead? Live?   (springing for so short time).
Look outside   from house, from head;
black bones of old twig,   leathery
last year's leaves   still underlie pink-
striped bunched buds,   the top ones
getting paler, taller,   bulging
upward as eye stares   for half hour,
minute   after minute, second, then
a following second.
        Get up! eye
was fooled by what   thought saw. Noon,
now, and petal's opening,   frills
falling outward until   edge is at
roof. Bang,
        bong. Bright, dark,
the drops hit   drummed-on metal;
bits of icy   hail, skittering,
shatter as storm   stops, starts,
crosses between   evaporating mists,
sun's flicker.   Out of, into, over,
farther off; whole   wheeling day's
passed by.   Who'll return, tomorrow (or
next year again   like last)
to see, ungone,   the good that we
could not believe in: joy
(junk hidden)   which proclaims
a future, whether   to any other eating
(eaten)   animal, or our own
ears,   mouths?

Galena Pass

Beyond Sawteeth,
valley of the snaking
ice-wide river   Past
stretches straight north,
its trappers and its wintry
beasts still known   may be
by green parks, the
aspen trees.
Tourists at an overlook
clicks view of far
years going away below
and finds, upright among   evil?
the pull-top tabs at
roadside, same
colony of blue   Future
beardtongue mountain-men
stomped on, Injuns
visioned, dying   at the last
pale-walled-imprisioned
I shan't
return, backpacking   won't come
toward my former
lovers, Jedediah,
holy-booked, or Crow   Now's
Killer, that old hoss, old
son: the grizzlies
of an earlier dream. But   whatever's

staring at sawn
teeth across
blue flower, I'll   hurting,
remember mountains
that will replace these
under more distant   reddening.
suns.

Sunbath

Leaf falls, bird
flies, white
butterfly flutters—
bees go buzz.
Perfectly
sun fits shade
(no gap)
and plum trees turn
from pale above
to drenched
stained-glass-at-evening
red below.
Meanwhile different
intentions of
chickadee (whizz)
gnat (wobble)
and (roaringly)
wind into,
through, out of
fir fronds
stitch all together—
I'll swear
my hot legs,
half-cooled hair,
belong here
within it too.

Madrone

Red naked dancers, madrone trees
bar view of fir-treed gorge, heat-
distanced hills. Across
the tilted scabland, air fall's
measured by a hawk. Foot
fumbling, hand clutched, human
camera's all. Home, we'll find
film error's left us only what
stayed behind eye: rust seedhead
against light, fern holed
in licheny crack, unknown
pink stars dotting along path
walked by a puma. Stone's weed
shall still stand here after both
wavering body and red forest
have been downed.

Bonobo's Garden

They say: that pygmy ape makes sex
do, for war; chimp matriarch and daughter send
their men off, bonded, to eat foreign devils'
evil up. On other hand, gorilla
girls leave, boys stay (mostly chastely) home
with mom. Among baboons, on tribal
march, old musclemen take center, with
their pregnant wives, ex-
pendable grannies limping to one side, while
teenage heroes, laden with testosterone, get
wasted on leopard. (See one boss man
making his woman carry dead fur
to its disintegration.) Above, below
volcanic ashfall, first family of humans step
out, their hidden footprints pacing
forward into time. Red—
headed mistress of the house of Sinn,
(Satann's daughter), which species
will you choose for archangelic tampering,
gene-change? to drain thought-heat
from skull, insert the virus that thins
finger to clutch more than stone, stumps
toe? Already Lucy,
under stars, carries a scavenged,
rot-filled hide before her, hangs on arm
in its long-hairy-tangled nest, or bag,
her child. Be sure, green

chitinous strangers, clicking your claws,
laws, that this flesh-world
has reached consensus, cell living within
cell, love-slave of lichen
riding its master. Blood
must recycle from those grinning teeth
through Tiger, into birth,
as food, future, shell—So
open! and let Kingdom
come.

Millrace

Fucking his lady duck,
the white drake fronts
her side, strokes head down
quickly, twice, then bills
neck feathers, shaking
soft snake out along ground
and climbs on, riding
that dark boat-body into
whatever weather. Surely
awkward tilt up
of the grey hips, down
of white, has to be done
with both of their desires
though only urgency above,
weakness of yielding under,
bring hole to hole (Leda's
excuse being lacked).
       Higher in air
swallows, like eagles
or albatross, meet after
a roller-coaster around,
around, chasing sky's
plane in threes, in
fours; the same mates
whose wings beat
closest together, caught
up in whirl (black/white

white/black) descend
like seed-winged samaras
doffed off of heaven's tree.
That jointure breaks
before ground's hit or
water billows.
      So do we here
flick on, off our own
comminglings as,
joining
we become
dizzied, bedazzled.

Entropy

Jay raised one young, this year;
(her/his) partner gone, alone,   Point
had to squawk twice as hard to teach
the stupid adolescent; cat, cat, cat   moves
(or man). In hiding still, not sure
except that momma, poppa is food's   banging
source, two different to call I
I (i)—tail crisp, crest jabbing   forward
out alone down. Old lady's feathers
straggle, by two seasons worn;   (yesterday's
she's got to see this last job done,   tomorrow's)
push child to its birth's (flight's)
pang. In house's window, looking to
leaves' light, no one may know   action,
if tree falls soundless, or which bird
flies out through winter, to reach   interaction
spring. That whisper-song   (of ions,
creature only years ago, has ended
as its destiny, a scream   changing
from predator or prey. So sun   chip)
that layers itself daily over night,
interlude; full Time compounds   computes
beginning with its Aim; lives, worlds
in a Lear's shout, a chaos   what's left.
boom. See, eye, reflection off of.

Sisters in Linnaeus' Garden

Species come and slide and go,   One cell's
mixing their parents, and without   fragments
known Begetter (except pollen
shed, brightness at petal, bee) always
too far apart to touch, too close   broken
for speaking, brother, sister, un-
acknowledgeable. Sight is what's   into
laid on soil that makes mind's
cells turn toward oddness, genes   bits:
(remembering wrong) to well
out hatred from our fox-fired   flowerings
greeneries again. Folks who kill (by
water, word, or pill) cry "hands   (of enemy, of friend)
cannot be trusted at the head" (as,
sisters, we gave only leg to lap). You, I   once
circled over telephone, munching
forth memory that was evermore   a new—
loved lie (those claimed
first angels, the devoured seeds   uprisen
from our half-emptied loaf). Why
has it got to be, this dirt,   (done, gone)
immaculate, a make-believe white
halo, around boxed-in brain? So skin
of fingers can taste (fed) again   at End.
the final kindness of Earth's
mothering bed?

The Specious Present of the Chickadee

Visitors, can you see through
my eyes, and by ears hear? ("Chick
tsk tseep"—which being   "Specious
imitated, you may disapprove and go.)
Just talk then, say "All things   Present":
OK": it's so. In greying grass,
at yellowed end of August (one   here fly
bird is back, then two, now three). The   chickadees—
rest of ten will be made up once
more, over next winter, as our
neighboring wood's flock passes   through future
life's sieve again. And those   toward past
I've loved? Having seen by
eyes of (young) and died with   (or, another
(older): gone. Can any presence use
such patterned cells for later   way?—
light? Know unskulled
world, or, earless, tremble? Hey!   Impossible!
you're brown-backed, chickadee
that somersaults, a whirling ball   not done)
around and round its insect-ridden
branch (tap, tick, "bark   making
pecker here") as center of a universal   geomorphic
limitless space-time. Who holds   line
stuck below your claw, a stick, now
dropped between leaves down   to flow
out of present. Past, Future, set

at spinning edge of circle
can be, have been, both an effect   (True
and its long-later cause, yo-   Dream)
yo-ing upon gravity's sink, where
essence becomes Be, right angle   curving toward
rounded. So, what is
sixth-sensed beyond   allowable
this narrow range we are   vision).
cut off alive in? ("Aroo, Arowr"
sings aging cat, knowing fate
hangs on her breath. "Tsk tsp tsert   You must
dee dee" 's reply.) Stop!   still!
the search; you cannot find   each Cause that's
answer until all   what it's caused by
that uses you has gone ahead,
leaving blind night   at edge
of Recollection.

Admonah

Adam (man of red clay) and Angel, in
same body's boat, quarrel over which end is
to go down first. (Your name, said Sabrah
friend, means "Red Bird, Burning" or
"Roast Goose," both made from unfound
meanings no field's action fits.) Under
sea's waters, or on layered earth, who will
grab iron, peg it into square holed truth? mis-
shape an emptiness, or unearth dust?
Stranger who's within me (is me?) runs from
being father's daughter into mother's ara-
besques, then faltering falls back on book's
mud-printed page, red-writ. The fired
clay's form (where storm's torn out glass
window pane, ten stories up, in black
Manhattan) lies cracked at foot. No mind
or matter but the bright electron's left, dug
out from that past hole, or (quickening)
gone on, alone, ahead.

Admonah (bird of red clay) is the Hebrew name of the tiny European robin.

Crow

My name is Crow and I'm alone;
the young one's gone for a new mate (my
old one left, somehow in snow, this winter
or the last). Rain crow! rain crow, just
one call that's longer that the time
between, measuring "no answer." Two
owls, last night, high gobble and a low
down boom, in passage. Through the graveyard
trees or over grass (anyone who eats her own weight
seven days a week [ten mice]
has to ride circuit.) Whereas I go for crumbs
and poisons, carrion in cans, not cleanly
as the hawks circling wing to wing above
the pine tops. Nor not in pools by imitation
river with its long hollowed
metal (feet on lucky pennies fallen in).
Ignored by flutterers through thorns,
I'm crow, and need more black-foreheaded
yard-wide-winged, brothers and sisters
past one old home of
crisscrossed branches in the fir tree tops,
to rise and circle between hills
and clouds. Hear! If there's any lonely, angry, proud
out there, from farther, closer, we must meet
together to remember our ancient crowing home,
or is it only shadow there in the tree top, hid.

Caddis

Caddis fly larva protects
soft skin, slime,   with bits
of sand, twigs.   Oyster (which
can secrete shell)   finds dirt
inside it hurts,   sculpts pearl.
Tall   man/woman mammal
piles trivia   (of red shift, black
holes)   around defenseless mind; if
that won't work,   sends song out,
blindingly.

AKA Evolution

Assuming that no one was God—could
whole creation bumble into ear, nose, eye
of human (deer, bacterium) from unaimed brain?
Filter out that noise of thunder, wave
spouted from sea bottom vent, stars falling
straight through space-flow: we've to leave
our traces in Earth's gassy breath. Time
having opened future, past, and Birth been
born (Death coming also, if all's still ahead) our
bleeding in clocked universe has commenced.
How shall this present playfulness, as of
child, pay back its ending, whether thorn or
nail? No one can know "I am It (Thou? That?)"
without fixed offer of self up through other: Tiger
saying "Here am I, your Buddha's body; eat"—
while the dissolving cells go off on own
to reabsorbence. Ignore such higher calling;
forego to be what's lighted, lit (a Lucifer
who slips down to, through, entropy, to zeero).
Accept, broke-boned, begetting into other
side of ether, where horizon's undiscovered edge
pulls whole in toward that central I
which is unfindable because there is
no place in which it's not.

Angel on Loop Trail

Red lava, coming down ten
centuries ago, stopped here.
Alighted on the chunky ridge
a seedling, stump
raises both arms, grey,
splintery, unfurling
inward to take-off. (Each
summer, climbing past, we've found
changes were in us, not it.) When
flow has covered land again, seeds
popped out from under to re-
colonize, new wings grown
from stone, we
shall be gone. Over smoking
stacks, downed on plain that hides
the stilling of man's wave, off-
spring of a hot-pot's
rust-eaten single cell grins
up at sky's cover, abstracting
cleanness, if to
no fire more. Unendingly,
sap aids erupted matter back
to its beginning.

Broken,

becoming,
a Human

sings

(only

Angels, leaves,
cry out
Joy);

worlds
(creaking,

chirruping)
continually

attune us toward

our oldest Aim.

Arboretum

Fractals of vine leaves, dark
against window, lightening
toward sun behind them, dim
to a sage shadow between
the layers they lie on. Whether
eyed as by maker, or unmade,
those serrations stubble
to sharp edge.
Fractals of black fir (cedar is
inset) entering the big-leaves, the
narrowed silver or poisonous rust,
arise to ascendancy, then fall
down mould's well.
River below, hear it, a rippling
of daylight, where overhead passage
of wide wings flows, shadow
varying its focus, in, out, from nest
toward roost, leaving
a terror-struck, emptied, long
path along stream. Hoo hoo
comes the summer night's
call, August
morning's yak yawk. Neither
ears nor eyes shall recover
from fractals until
made part of hill's whole, an unending circle.

Even the parents of swim-suited
children, or old folks wheel-chaired,
proceed on same curving
time-line (leash-guided, mutt-
dogged), conform
to perfection
of fragmental whirl.
Suddenly, now, the green fruits
on stems purple,
as their boughs turn
toward cold.

Patagonia

The peaks of Pai'ne   can be seen
one day in ninety   un-cloud-wrapped;   Eternal
standing *penitentes*,   topped
each by ice hat,   they've split   balance—
apart, air,   shafting down
four thousand feet   to a dumb   joy's
plain, one hand,   glaciers calving
into shadow sea   the other. Sun   quick,
yellows the oncoming   heaped-up shroud
across Atlantic,   sets reddening   wrath's
western fog.   Let camera people
jounce in photo'd   car   long;
past straits of fire   their dead-
line's north).   Impossible   equal
brooding figures   wait, covering
stone faces   under year's   load,
long storm   till that odd calm
when, blindingly,   end   upraised.
of continent's   lit.

Typhoon

Crash; confound all; down with houses, trees and world;
only the quiet fat man weeps at branches menacing his lives.
I laugh: Indoors the sky is screen, as flesh is, to the fire storm.
Beyond air, and spirit, and the thin quick stupid film of life,
reigns turmoil and will reign the cold. Old knowledge
we inherit and refuse, our eyes on higher things, on the divine
lacery of nerves' thought; on cinematic scorings of what is,
to freezing or to crackling cells, a happy interlude.
Too grave and understanding of the issue here,
a seeing of the flash from downswept wires, the ambulance before
all other houses than your own, the blankness that observes
what's coming on, is a defect. Unmannerly, who will
not live while living's good, or in the peaceful center of the storm
hug arms to his immunity? The flooded air
made thick by hurricane with long sticks of trees, if it could
cut down through our clothed minds, would we admit
we wished it? Only the fat, gentle man, the one with
wife and children on the brain, gnaws fingers at the telephone.
We others rampage in a room of empty habits, of shelter from
the furor and the outside wail; we let ourselves have hate
and even excitation, to be sure we move.
Thus if you would avoid the sin of asking evil
you must try to go on through the chill outside thin skin,
a touch of which stops all. See, say, what's fatal to you
and by a little death slow long. Inoculated,
coward child and grand, obtuse adult wait sober for the
gates to open, light to be closed down. This wind

is neither frivolous nor wrong, that brings remembrance
to us in the fallen-out boughs, that stirs
two who condemned each other to cross hands, leaves
the uxorious man, his home and fir trees intact in his arms,
a half life nearer to the last unclasping by this one
day's prayer. I, blinking, have acquired the thought
of where the wind goes when it quits out there.

Beardtongue

"If I was a penstemon," I said, "I'd
grow here," and stepped off
into inlet of trees, mainly
to tell truth, for a chance
to be alone in bush. Far
in, farther beyond view: the men
gone by now. Turned round—
under bracken and salal, in dense
brush of ditch, bright
leaves circle, purple head waves:
"Come look, it's us. A million years
we've waited on hillside
for someone to talk to, a lover
who'd say not 'this is mine' but
'I'm its.'" Naming myself
for self's discovery, I had
no thing beside me then,
but friend.

I Am What That Horizon Says to Me

Penstemon Cinicola

Incarnate

Begin with a baby, as
every good book should   Sun
(of world, of man);
end after mountain   booms,
crossing, at the first, last
sea. Put people   within
onto pages, add   the unheard
odd bits of fragile
butterfly designs, deep   sound's
holes for blazing
dark-winged worms. Then   white
when moon's light's up, striped   wave
Tiger roars, and Hero
(young baboon, old granny)   (differenced,
comes out of tribe, dies   made
to save us, evermore.   a Word)
No one shall claim
we are not, now   in wind's
or later, all so called
down into dust, to feed.   annulling.

Creationism

Red Spider Woman's
rock, that can't be got
up, has blue necklace
thrown down on top. Put
there before helicopters, says
pick-up truck guide, black-
hatted (without cocoon,
not piton-hung or webbed,
no banging overnight against
stone face, no bad
hardware, no hands).
Made maybe on spot
by thunder, story goes, sun
clasped. Or did
old big-armed priest,
early in unlit walls
of canyon (quick-
sand wash, grassed
belly from which She
rises, and her Speaker,
into noon) fling arrow
over silhouetted
needle, center's pole?
Like spiderlets, treading
moony threads into
upper air, it went
higher, like dark

water under fall, down;
more string and more
pulled after, yucca-
fiber bead cord. Heaving,
huh-huhing: up clunks chain,
catches light for ever
after. (But how'd
singing get rope to
come down? Human cause
cut from its effect-
how was turquoise
circled, spread?) Magazine
photoing amateur
friction-climb, fly boys'
shake of heaven's
beam, allows gift
was left to let Whitey
home whole. Fact's
now lost, unfit
for believing. Spider
Woman, who wove
all of it, even to missing
link, is laughing
a pebble off.

Darkly

There is no word for color light comes through;
the green, rust, brown of glassy leaves around
opaque blossom, or wet stalk that flicks
like unseen aircraft, on off-on; blue
snail-shell's shine. Dirt we can say; its grey
takes in each, giving back none. But (ground
to bolt), without such stop the spark
of universe could neither flare nor die; our clayey
mother, matter, hides more sun than
her sky shows. Glow's got to be on cloud,
God (by some) eyed; a world that is unhulled's
unknown.

Paradigm, Shifting

World outside window gives through skull
Word-talk to isolated dreamer, dier, though   Words'
this polleney web-coated screen (of the eyes'
lids) can not bring meaning into, out of   meaning's now
sound. I am what that horizon says to me,
do as am told, returning from all other
selves to oldest goal: "From Me to   our Goal:
Me" was what God also ordered, incarnate.
(Correct? That is the act we're here to wait for,
be?) Do not let mind's wells go dry; but   a becoming
where thought's track is tracing, winds
must cease, sun stop its stepping through and through   (outside all
our eyes, heart, hair; a corruscation. So
I assume, that hand, this head I feel on million   beings',
shoulders, is my own, serving for greenery. Brain
does not allow the separation of its presences
(as atom, joining on the left, on right; or moving   atoms'
into a day's dancing). Shall voices, yours and mine,
come into focus at this incandescent, irid-
escent face, between our airy glass, our lake-like   moving)
waters? If quieted, what my brown eyes see   shown
reflected from below, is your blue-green, or in ear   near
above) a twitter of paired nuthatches, tittuping, up   where
down tree. Here my stopped tongue must make   Word's
on its own-uncountable, the word-wide worlds. Never!   speech
break surface betwccn sought-out, seen, that
hoped-for raising, lowering of our holy   (hoped-for)

lie (of lived-in loss, of died-for loving) where   meaning's
neither I nor other's more than a reverberation   dying.
within black ether's matter.

Points, Time Framed

Not in words, show
birds, or as
red, round wood; that   Thin
leaves out air, time
and scream.
Tootling of horns
gives belly's burning   Future
not mind's. Oldbeat
in memory movie, eagle
circles, gull
yells; wind upwelling   brightening
over graveyard, chutes
down to town.
That motion omits
watcher's wish, preyed-   (into
on's prayer, sky'd
eyer: what's
known in all three's   now,
bones. Even
a sparrow, weakening
attacker, spun
above, below   dims,
yo-yoing, yammering
at raptor,
can not rupture
string between them
of hate's love, heat's inner

cold,   flickers.
unto; unseen.
We hold
no flattened, emptied soul's
reconstituted
except by act   entering
that puts it (lacking) into
ugly fact.
You are not   past.
You, rebirthed
but other earth.

Time's Arrow

Mind, finding its drug (dream),
brings back our left-hand's heaven
inside bone. Mouth watering at
word of fool, ear thunders (as tear
jerks). Now waking out of
old embrace, can sorrow still be
blinded by soon opening eye (our I?)
to how each risen sun goes down
toward its day's westering? So
shall hope, squeezed out through
chasmed histories, allow this
tongue to sing its folly (of love, of
hate, of hand's trying to reach other
hand) a push of meaning through that
final end, found under sun's set (I? me?
we? who is, are, will be, You?)
The plain of future, opening out, past
our passed ends, ahead we see
time's arrow, once again, as what
is always farther on than
where it's at.

The Gaudy-Mouse
For two Emily's, Carr and Dickinson

Sun sets blue/pink, or
orangey maroon; rock
gets in shoe. A woman   Soul.
has to be crazier than a man
for paint to swirl
into shape for her; stymied
by ugly Act. Why is   cross-
incarnation (of ape's sight
into word) (of smiling
child to bed-hulk,   stretched
bottom or side paralyzed, one
eye white) (or the dream
working its way out   over
through stone, against the
hammerer's hands) what breaks,
as well as makes,
world? Extraordinary how   Nothing,
little difference in tone,
or face moving, changes
postcard to be a framed
view, person,   upholds
as "I". The party dress
of stars and rivers
we are seen in, burns
up close, floods away,   all
a dust. Maybe
crookedness and clatter,

smoke, were wanted,
(not needed) by God, as
fighting back better; Stuff   is.
standing on own.

An Alan and an Ann

Web with center everywhere
has no edge to it; circle   Who?
being endless others, one,
one, and one. See how friends   unseen,
get older, gone, the same   done, then
face returning, here as Alan,
there, an Ann. (I'm   none.
waiting to make tree, grass blade,
or long wild cat, when   Whose?
atoms rearrange). Fore,
aft, the time dimensions aren't   (not mine)
distinguishable from east,
west, north, except   doomed,
if Cause is (knowledge known,   looming
Eve aimed). Unzip, zip,
the cell becomes its own   (comet,
seed, womb, home, a   killed—
hole's blackening, or sun gush   joy's blast?)
of light through whiteness.
Toward, behind, in; that   millionth-of-an-
evolution is named (by   instant
one friend) Chance, by   second
other) God. Yet if   Bang's
woven across newer warp, we
may find one-on-one again,   upcoming:
that, added into Two,
make worlds.   a Word.

Deer Park Again

Flowers dance, as shown
by their motionless edge's
ruffles, after, before, they bend.
Framed, eye fills what's
empty, voids the full; un-
remembered, as it has been, so
will be. Soon separated
(all towards love, hate) souls
grow (kill, eat, open into
seeds - dry, go). Combine?
to be again what was, without
change: then there's no thing, time,
or whirl. Bang becomes,
if soundless, two ends
of a black (white) hole,
new-born or buried. See
green grass's flame, in eyes
that blink on, off. Buddha's
the transparency, unseen,
between.

Whole's

(hole)—

now

(no one's)
Icon that

can't be

seen:

an I

mirroring
Universe's
Eye.

Eucaryote

The old woman said to the young one, why   (One,
go doubled, bent over like me? You've   Two'd)
no excuse. As long as the pixillate eye peers   fearing,
and the smile, out under hat, we've each   deformed
got something to go on, Selves. Who here
lets sound of rivers fade, glitterings, hidden,   by hatred,
prune back into pain? Weaving
the nod, bow, lift-of-hand dance at   lovers
dinner-plate party (bonobo's rite) shouldn't
all play again this one-into-everyone game?—See-ers   who were
through eon of humans, or listeners, may touch   never
eternal tinkle and brightness. Yet   unaimed at
only the splendid amoeba remains, welcome   (Single)
in waters, coming lonely down times   reach
fully-fleshed, flesh unchanged. Glassy-eyed,
gutted, the ranked, racked antlers
(snooty above us in Elks'? elks'?   any-
touristy hall) overlook shooting, get shot   where?
by hunters, eating feast of proud food.   here.
So virus, living commensal in creatures
(old aunty, grandchild) becomes again   (Two'd,
part of life's cell, being us (we, soon,   earthed)
being it) body, brain twinned
(walled, untwained) to sun's grave, forever   home
together at end.   (One'd)

Curve

Ellipses circle, bearing planet
beads, orange, grey, greenish-blue and red.
We know parabola returns, as comet
has come by, to birth and death a man. Yet
here stands tree in air, its arms
throwing hyperbole at sky: without
a prayer. And no spot is not so. What
gives? Do this wired world's lives'
lines lead? Mute, center that is everywhere
sends bent radius out toward a there:
unending end, not gone.

Lykewake

We wake the body of world's partying,
who bouse its booze. And where does
that corpse wake? Lucky if as bunch
of leaves on branch's end, a hand of
ovals opened out to light, transmitting
green below. Who'll say which
life is higher, or if landfill's dust
may serve same function, to a Buddha's
eye, as matter hid in ether, black or clear.
While I have an I, it can't have found
if such seen glow persist, when See-er
changes to far side of bone, and long
Withins must follow our short
Outs.

Artwork

Flower fell, from sky's light
past sun-through-green, behind
the whitening shadows of ten-
mouthed (each five-frilled) trusses
down to be browned
on ground—a drip of rain
then added. If one could hold
such spots within some air-like
acrylic block, transparent,
where a moving eye or odd
searchlight might activate
it, what
joy for the artist (God?)
who does
exactly that.

Credo

God that has been's kind;
Who is now, knows,   Truth's
and Mary, Holy Ghost, can
bring anything to birth; but these   gotten
three shall not join till time
turns One, whose good   here
is powerful, existence loving, in-
finite choices wise.   by pain;
Meanwhile we weep for Him
who's torn, being bodied   Perfection
in our earth for mere tears,   wants
joys. Outside of universe
such Passion has no Ground.   Growth.

Lithofragma (Saxifragaceae)

Over done body, the Rock-breakers rise   Bright
Petaled; shouldering our mountain's knees,
foam fisheres slide, eroding earth's main   beings'
toward sea. We'll flatten grandly plains
of storied memory bearing, after the robots   buzz
and before ice age, same seed. Doffed
shell around brain's flower, fading,   (into an inemptiness
sinks back bed. My love, the Universe
of ant, of crow, of burst-bark leaves   beneath)
still shows translucence filling all
up to the skin-brinked eyelids well.   still
Yet we've a darker end, must get
to out last holes far side, unwomb   what is
creation there and (unregenerated)   here
tomb.   homed.

Link

Death being based on life, and no birth
without a burial (Bang ending always in
sky's hole) animals and earths must
carry both as one cross, em-
bodied. Without new day's faded
memory of old (mouse skull
shaken out of compost, six months after
trap caught it) is no time, no causal
press of leaf against tree bark, flutter
of mouth, mothlike, on eyes' lids,
all, wholed.

Praise,
Pain:

(minused,
a Zero)

(summed up,

One)

Rain Cycle

Only bone, skin meet at rim
between soul's wells. As fox,   Bright
mouse's eye, share tooth sap
out of one into other's skulls, veins   iris, red
channeling, you, (I) come
to each stone trodden (shard   stained
nimble held)—never on axis,
always other where (as is   both
kindness of humans, a cat's
grin, mayfly hopefulness) from   east, west
home. Shape taken after Bang, dim   (night long)
birth (of quartz stars, Coal Sacks,
around which swing infinity's   silvery
waters), Earth's dogged Sun's   ringed moon
circling. Opposing
nesters (chicka-dee-dees, the crows)   whether
yammer not at neighbor
but at viewer, bug danglers'   silent
whoosh or always into evening
holes—small anes' popping   (whisper
(to this spot? That?) bar
us folk out of wished-for   "Aurora") or
left behind, bed under river by each
new bunch of ten-year-old   unbending
replaceable forever (rain,
stream, ocean, cloud
and again rain) You, We,   going down

leave now not found, that
center which is every where,
but no one's at.

Editor's note: In the context of astronomy, "Coal Sack" may
refer to a dark nebula so named, whose dust particles obscure
light from Milky Way stars behind it.

Other

Winking under change of light, stone   Inertia
head stays dead, as white that flowed
bloodless over sculptor's apron, arms   then,
set to be plaster. Where in man's
narrow bone can he get room   now
for flesh-fruit, spirit? Friend
who called self body's potter worked   action;
on lives like clay, lost own. Now having
made of our beginning, end,   far off
unready yet to hide old selves
in penetrated ground, we quick look off   ahead,
at worldly blue and green, claim
that which causes joy is found   Soul;
within. Triad of clod, moved; breath-
smothered dier's frenzy; a womb's gift of
shape to nothing, make our senses'   outside,
fence to open. How rarely skin
is troubled by those hands, announcing
the non-self, the more than maker, shows   timelessly,
but one act is usable, in lives,
that mind find   Other.
brother.

Finger

Did finger, stirring once, infect
void's bubble with its weight,   Lacking
noise, light, or is blame
longer lasting—what, Immanences   before,
still there? The crazed
corners, folds of inner into outer   after,
(lone to mind, as the galactic
stream to its bacterium, Earth) allow   Nothing
an O of hope. From
busyness of the reached now   is heard,
not just black future's hole
but past (Time's snake, Tail   seen;
mouthed) must wall us around.
Blows wind blooms chasm, blasting   All
against non-being's one-hand   emptied,
clap—the interference
that creates, from first,   our world's
last aim. No who
beyond that's needed,
or is found.   One.

Legacy

Saying is what counts, not	Noise
being heard. Perhaps to	
carry on world's life	(even not
into some other future is	
our one job—to turn course	rhymed)
around while holding still	
a mother's (father's?) hand	can't
or fetus's (as I did once	
but not a second time) can	make
be achieved by circling	
just beyond what's lacked:	Truth,
Belief. How may failed	
human, on third planet	if
(built, as he, she, always was,	
from bad clay's mud) endure	pains
through our oncoming	of
starless night? See	
prisoners in tunnel dig past	our dying
blocked eye-slit to find	don't.
way up, by (if lucky) roots	
at the closed end. Through	Losing
blackest light (once known	
to Greeks as ether, matter,	(long-lost)
now our newest minds'	eyes'
confabulation) out of those	bright
trillion dimensions we've	
become adults to play with	hold

(though living in just one): Time   allows
is, as unseen as the emptiness
encircling our worm's hole,   no grace,
an arrow speeding forward toward
each egg, every womb. We
share what was, again will be   no meaning
after earth's ending, with
the dinosaur, the cell. Do not   beyond
(as chimp, bonobo, or elephant
knowing ancestral bones)
fail test. Have what's called   Song.
Faith. Go on.

Day's Light

Same river ran full flood, no   Outline
banks, no source, how'd fish
head up? Undimmed, light's flashes   had to
blind, eyes being stopped
by their own opening. If flow   shape
of atoms does not turn one particle
to hit another, hate, or kill,   wholc;
love's undiscovered. Bond
bounds, as knowing proves   pain's
knowns little, or earth lives
in us by dying: mud, that holds   the skin,
to grass, melts in seed's rot,
coats dust. That fruit   the husk,
which ended paradise was brain,
or nucleus, or quark. Sun's   outside
clod, hiding our unending hoped
for night, must darken what it   a Soul.
makes light.

March Window

When eye can no longer see
Gods in March leaves, ear
hears trees entering wind,
know Orion's
strides the night, through Sun's
unclouding show us
noon—how can square built
words be used as bricks
to make a body's house
be home! Thud on the bone
of cancelled leg, or mud
hold mend, we got to go
out toward feared door, find
something of a light at end
of the remembered tunnel, a
way up forward, or run
back to womb. Ponch
of flesh softens, as black
ness forms form. Where,
when to report it? What's
proof beyond each cells
own lies? Yet, scene
seen beforehand (or, after,
turns later to be true)
is all that any I can
know: at one, at two, shoot
upward, at ninety, close

the lid which opened ends
shut. Whenever after
comes (in instant of
eternity? Now's longing
a last flickering flutter?) all
one's to see is: memories
that turn out to be futures,
reminders (Hells. Heavens?)
of last fall's field of
leaves, in full sun,
soon to come.